SECRETS
TO HITTING
MORE JACKPOTS

THESLOTGURU

To order additional copies of this book, contact:
Xlibris
1-888-795-4274
www.Xlibris.com
Orders@Xlibris.com

To order additional copies of this book, contact:
Butterman, LLC
Fax 1-888-540-8790
www.theslotguru.com

ISBN: Softcover   978-1-4628-5560-5
         Hardcover   978-1-4628-5561-2

Library of Congress Control Number: 2009908332

Print information available on the last page

Rev. date: 08/30/2019

My experience with TheSlotGuru. . .

What an experience it was. It was something that I wasn't expecting. Once he told me where we were going. I was ok with that but he didn't tell me that this was going to be a big shock of my life. Once we pulled up and valet took the car, I already at that moment knew that he turned into a different person. His game face was on. I still do not know what I'm in store for. It was a beautiful place, soon as we went over to the slot machines, he pulled out his $. I knew it was something different. He didn't pull out $20; he pulled out $8000 in $100 bills. He put his first 100 on, he played for 5 minutes and off of a few hundred $ he hit twice on two different machines. He tried to give me as much attention as possible but he was focused. He went around the casino to different slot machines, having lights go off as often as he could. Where ever you see the lights going off at he was there.

The casino workers showed him so much respect. I can tell that they knew him very well and this was something that he does a lot. I have never seen something like that before. It's almost like TheSlotGuru turned into a different person. He still was very humble but he still had greed about him that was very different.

Some people go just for fun, No! This is serious work for him. It's not a hobby; it's a lifestyle for him. He told me, "You have to spend $ to make $." I slowly realized that. He had very little to do emotion on his face. He was very intense. He had the whole attention of the casino. Everybody wanted to be next to him or play the machines that he was on. I noticed that when he played, he never once looked at the screen. He stayed looking around or at the light.

He will play 7 to 8 machines at one time. I was so amazed. He was there on a mission and he was going to make that mission and no matter what was cost. He's not the one to just give up. He's a true go getter. But, he always stayed very respectable. He showed everybody from the other players to the attendants with the most respect. I enjoyed my experience with him. It was the first time I have seen anything like that and I don't think I ever will because every time I see the lights go off back to back, at different machines, at different times, it was very amazing to me. It is not even like he is paying me to do this. No! I didn't even know that this lifestyle was a part of him. The reason why I decided to write is because I wanted people to know what it was like to look in as this was taking place. It was an amazing experience that a lot of people would not get a chance to see.

INTRO

I must congratulate you on one of the most powerful decisions you will make in your life pertaining to slot machines. Now, before I get started I must tell you that every single word, phrase or thought in this book is of my own opinion!

All of these ideas that may seem basic are my own thoughts and I'm only giving you something to think about or experiment with while gaming! And if you decide to use any method or modes that you are about to read will be of your own free will neither I or my affiliates or my sponsors are not responsible for your bad out come (that's the gamble)! Please don't play with money you can not afford to lose…. remember the casino is a business! I want to pass on information the everyday person can use, because I am an everyday person!

I also want to note that some of the things you are about to read may sound kind of contradictory, and too simple to be true, well as your reading you are also looking at my real photos I took when I won. Please pay special attention to the dates on the photos, take it from someone who is doing it, night in and night out. Yes, there are a lot of things in everyday life that's a contradiction….if you read the book enough times, you will soon get into my way of thinking and you will be enlightened to see my *mindset* and my way of thinking inside the casino (and outside as well)…the only thing that's bound to happen if you re-read my book is, you will find something different to take with you to the casino on your next trip, every time! Everything that you will read in this book, I use in my gaming strategy! Trust me

I have read a lot of books on the market by all types of people, so called employees of casinos and different people that claim they know how to hit the slots at the casino and they claim they can tell which slot is going to hit. Believe me, if people could hit so often, why not work full time at it, like I do if they're hitting so well! The bottom line is you not only got to have heart to play slots for a living, you also have to be a little crazy! Well the information that I'm putting out in my book is coming from a person that has done it and still doing it, my friends! It was total rubbish and it hurt me to read such non-noteworthy information the other people put out, so I had to do something! I did, I wrote my manual on how I'm doing it (*the real deal*)…… Welcome to my world of gaming my friends! Yes you! Come follow me.

I started to play slots nineteen years ago, when I was stationed overseas in Germany. Once I was discharged from the army (*honorabl*e discharge of course), I started working for the government and playing the slots around my home town in Michigan... Until I started making more money at the slots than at my job, so I relinquished my job (yes I did,) and I'm a professional slot player (with no regrets at all), it's how I make my living! I would not advise anyone on doing that! Unless you start hitting like me! And can afford to take some losses, my friends…

So I decided to write a real book! From a real person! For real people who want to win *real* money! Also make a note that if anyone tells you that you're going to be successful at the casino all the time… he/she is a liar! Be prepared to lose and win! That's where the fun is …to just win all the time make me nervous…I have to lose a little, to appreciate my winnings… And if you're really good you will leave while you're ahead. But that's rare, most of the time when we are winning we tend to hang around trying to win more…when in most times, there is no more to win *that night*! But that's the gamble my friends…

I think I'm most qualified to write this book because I have done it night in and night out. And I'm still doing it! Setting lights off in every casino I go in! I'm not bragging my friends, yes it's a rush that only a person that has been able to get a light to go off can understand, and if you have then you know exactly what I'm talking about. And if you haven't, well I'm going to show you how I did it! When the light goes off, I never know how much I won, because my style of play is, *I don't* look at the screen when I play (*Max* bet of course). That's right, I do not look at the screen of the game or games I'm playing. I look at the different slot machines around me. I look at the people around me. I'm standing most of the time so after each hit of *Max* bet, I glance at the light on the top of the machine. What a RUSH it is when that light goes off!!!!!! It has been times when, I would have a light going off and I would ask a total stranger to look at the screen and tell me the winning combination! I then try to figure out what I won before I look at the screen or I would ask a stranger to tell me how much i won, it is truly exhilarating... Ahh, one can never get enough of those lights, those lights, those red, white or blue lights...

DISCIPLINE IS ONE WORD YOU SHOULD GET TO KNOW

You will have to be very disciplined to play slots whether they are high limits slots or the penny slots. You must be disciplined enough to walk away when you are ahead but also remember that you want to win, so it will be your call... In my opinion if the machines stop hitting or get cold and don't pay out, walk away and play another machine, then come back and play it for a few rounds, if still nothing then leave it alone and don't look back! 'Cause someone may come up as soon as you get off the machine and hit it! So it's best not to look back! If that should happen, then you congratulate the person that hit and move on, I guarantee you karma will be on your side, my friend...if not that day another day.

Congratulations! Another Winner!

$18,030.00
January 10, 2009

$36,000.00
June 11, 2009

$18,000.00
June 11, 2009

Remember you are in the casino to have fun first and foremost! Never forget that simple rule. Yes, I know we all want to win and win big, but we must first understand that we will never break the casino rules; that being said, go and have fun playing slots and watch how your game changes if you have what I call slot etiquette.

1) *RESPECT THE ELDERLY NO MATTER HOW BAD OF A TRIP YOU ARE HAVING. ALWAYS HELP THEM, MOVE THINGS, OBJECTS OUT THEIR WAY IF NEEDED, PUT THE ELDERS' NEEDS IN FRONT OF YOUR OWN EVEN IF YOU ARE LOSING*!!!!!

2) Never argue over a machine with anyone.

3) Never hit on the slot machine or slam the arm on the one arm bandit.

4) Play with the strategy of thinking outside the box! I don't do the norm! I do the opposite of the "so called norm", whatever that is!

5) Blend in with your gaming surroundings. And have a blast win or lose!

6) *GIVE BACK!!!! YES THESLOTGURU IS SO SURE YOU ARE GOING TO START HITTING I WANT MY CUT, THAT'S RIGHT... BUYING THE BOOK WAS MINIMAL COMPARED TO WHATS COMING YOUR WAY. AND I WANT MY TENTH. YOUR KARMA WILL CHANGE IF YOU DON'T COMPLY WITH THESE SIMPLE RULES.THE INFORMATION I'M GIVING YOU WILL BE WORTH AS MUCH TO YOU AS IT IS TO ME*

 Because if you actually look at a person that hit and/or bang on slot machines or swear at machines they really don't have karma on their side. And let's not forget it's a machine!!! It would be best not to play too close to that type of individual. That's my experience when I run across those types of slot players I keep my distance.

Thinking out the box meaning, don't always play the same games, go to different games and I always play *Max* bet! I play a lot of the games that has bonus rounds. The pay off after a good bonus game could be a wonderful experience with life changing money as well!

Again *Max* bet is the name of my game and bonus games pay me well…that's if I'm playing the penny, nickel, dime, quarters and dollar machines and above.

Playing higher limit slots can be a bit more intricate… you must first start off with a sizable bankroll! Please don't expect to go in high limits with 100 or 200 dollars and expect to be successful on a consistent basis! On a few occasions you can set a light off with a small bankroll, most of the time when you step to high limits, you should have a sizable bankroll. Don't get me wrong, all it takes is one pull in high limits and you can walk out ahead, but remember we are talking about casinos and they are not there to make every Joe and Mary wealthy! That being said, when you step to high limits you, in my opinion "should have at least one thousand dollars" and that's on the low side. Your trip would go a lot better on the dollar machines and below which is not a problem because they also pay well, my friends! That's enough to play quite a few rounds on the slots and if you lose, then it won't cost you your house and car and if you hit well, you will be happy to say the least! You take my advice and follow the steps that I share with you that have given me great success over the years with no *fake s*tories. It's all about being the best gamer you can be…if you master *one* of my techniques you will be a happy person. Now read on so I can get my cut once you start making the lights off …

Once I step on the high-limit floor, my mind and thoughts are on *lights.* Nothing more nothing less. I don't play for credits on a slot machine, I play for the *light* on the *top* of a slot machine to go off. And believe me its not hard to do a few times, but to make a light go off every time you go to a casino, well that's more of a pro and that's what I am, my friends! And if you follow the information I put out in this book you will be able to set *lights* off' not only on your next visit but every visit! The lights come on when you hit a winning combination for one thousand two hundred dollars or more on one spin. Ahh! that's what I play for the bright lights, the pretty bright lights! And that's what this book is about and what my mindset is on every time I enter a casino...the pretty white or sometime light blue lights on top of the slot machine. You purchased this book for a reason and if you follow my advice I'm sure you will be successful at the casino more times than otherwise. Remember *leave when you are ahead* - the result from not observing this simple rule can cost you your whole bankroll before you decide to leave.

You always want to play with what you can afford to lose. Always! I never play with money that I have to pay a bill with but then again I live a cash- only lifestyle so I really don't have any bills. I will say things in this book; multiple times for a reason...saying things back to back and often is a good learning tool. I swear by it! Your job is to pick up on the multiple things I repeat. Learn them. Study the statements I make in this book, take them to the casino with you, and watch how enlightened you will become, my friends...

To me there are a lot of playing styles out there, but for now let's concentrate on two types of (easy to miss) playing styles....one style is for the person who goes to the same casino often and the other is for the person who goes to any casino only a few times a year. If you go to the casino two or three times a year, then you need to put this book down...no don't refund it just put it down... I'm just kidding, I hope you enjoy the information that I'm putting out. And for the ones that go more often and even for the ones that don't go that often, let's take a trip into the life of a professional slot player. I'm going to be brutally honest and realistic in these passages. I do believe in *the lord*. That being said, I do pray while I play slots (sometimes), some people claim that it's wrong to gamble, (maybe so, maybe no) but if you look hard enough ,you can find something wrong *with* everybody, my take on people that say you shouldn't gamble is *mind your business*.. Because the same people that want you to stop when you lose will be the same people with their hand out once you win. I'm going to take you into my world of gaming my friends enjoy...

Congratulations! Another Winner!

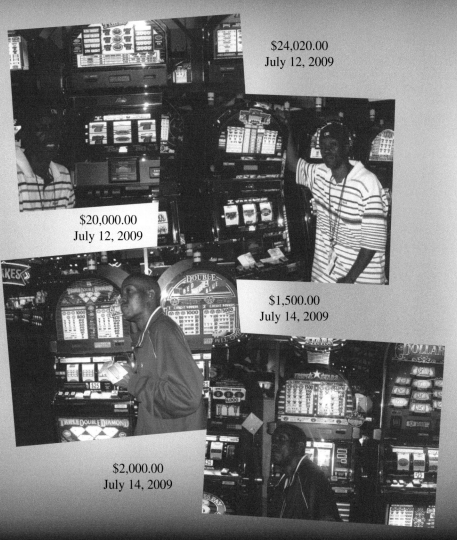

$24,020.00
July 12, 2009

$20,000.00
July 12, 2009

$1,500.00
July 14, 2009

$2,000.00
July 14, 2009

WHAT'S ON MY MIND WHEN I'M ENTERING AND WALKING INTO THE CASINO!

Attention to detail; as I walk through the casino on my way to high limits, I'm always looking around for those blinking lights! If for nothing else, I'm looking for the area the lights are going off in and making mental notes on that area (no particular machine just the close area). Then later that night or one day in the future, I'm going to play in those areas. Just the idea that the lights are going off lets me know the casino is paying someone and that's a good feeling to *TheSlotGuru*. On my way to my slot section, I hear people on the card table hollering for twenty- five bucks they just won... I look, smile and keep on moving towards my area with lights on my mind. The card tables and dice tables bring out a lot of intensity from people that make them scream and shout! The slots also have a way of making a person scream or shout as you will find out! Moving on...

Once I arrive in the high limit area, I scope the area, then if there aren't any lights going off, I then go and try to make *some* go off. First I look for the highest paying machines; I *Max* bet and hope for the best!!! I don't believe there is any way a person can tell when a machine will hit (unless you are playing the machine and it has paid you a nice sum of money and something inside you feels as though you should continue), nor can they determine which machine will hit by what is on the screen when they walk up! There are times, however, that you will be on a machine and you can just feel it will hit and in fact it will...not all the time but it does happen...

And if there are lights going off in your gaming area be sure to remember which machines (or area around machine) are lighting up. Some people that win collect their winnings and leave without really putting any money back into the machine they just hit and they move on. I say go behind them and put some cash not a lot of cash in there ...about 100bucks is OK. Remember you're in high stakes! If you're on the penny machine do the same thing but insert 20bucks or 50bucks if your bankroll can take it! If you don't play that day on your next visit try the machine that you seen with the lights going off, you may be pleasantly surprised! It doesn't matter how much it hit for sometimes they do hit back- to -back or even back- to - back - to - back! That is one of the biggest thrills for me, not knowing when or if a machine will hit repeatedly... that's the gamble, my friends...

All of the styles and techniques I'm about to discuss with you in this book will not be able to be accomplished in one visit to the casino not even a hundred visits. Pick a few techniques that I will give you and put together your very own personal style and try them on one visit. The more you read on the more complex my gaming will get, so catch your breath and get ready to follow me as I make those lights go off....oh yeah one more thing, I will not be telling you any gimmicks I'm going to be giving you my exact movements, my thoughts and pictures and my 1099s(tax forms) before, after and during my game play. So if you read and get a good understanding of your reading ,you will uncover your own style of play. Happy reading my friends...............

"REMEMBER BUT FORGET"

Yes, my friends, that's what *TheSlotGuru* does... if I made a lot of money at the casino one trip, it's good to know you did it, but as soon as you walk back on the gaming floor the next trip you must try to forget the past and start thinking about the future of your success which is here and now ,my friends... I can't specify enough that the "here and now factor" must be implemented on a regular basis. For your success to have longevity don't get caught up on your last trip; it could be a fatal error! Good or bad, I try to forget the last trip and start fresh as I go in. Then you may get on a game that was not hitting on your last trip and play it. To your amazement it may bring you a light! Max bet of course....

"ALWAYS BE POLITE"

Yes, this is true, always be polite whether you are winning or losing, I truly believe in karma. Or just treating people with common courtesy seems to go a long way with my karma in the casino and out. Many times I have been uplifted by strangers in good moods.... When I wasn't doing so well at the casino on certain nights, just a simple "hello" or "having any luck buddy?" seemed to have changed my luck a few times. I don't like to talk to much until I win, which brings me to my next topic...........

TALK WHEN YOU FEEL LIKE IT!

 It may seem simple enough, but you will be surprised at how many people want to talk to you when you're gaming and making lights go off. To *TheSlotGuru* this can be an annoyance. It's best to stay focused and keep your mind on gaming using your very own technique and not to be side- tracked by idle chatter; nothing wrong with speaking but idle chatter while you're trying to make thousands!!!!!!!! talk if you feel like it…tell them to get this book! Thanks for the promo…

"ALWAYS HELP THE ELDERLY"

Although I'm in the casino to get money, I can't help but see elderly people with their walkers or oxygen tanks. First I think it's awesome - they are out enjoying themselves trying to win money or anything for that matter is a competitive obsession and to see my elders out competing is fantastic! I look at each elderly person like they are my grandparents! (they don't know that's how I look at them and that's okay because I know some of them look at me as their grandson.) I take it upon myself to move a chair for them or clear an aisle for them or if I'm smoking and someone of age sits next to me, *I put it out*! No questions asked. Then if I see them light up a smoke, I light up and only then, my friends. Even if I'm in the smoking area it doesn't matter, I either don't smoke or I go to another machine! I wouldn't want my grandparent around cigar or any kind of smoke, would you? Of course not. Yes treating people right is a part of my gaming experience and I favor older people who are at the casino gaming!!!!!!!!

"HIGH LIMITS"
(the cats meow!)(or the THESLOTGURU'S Retirement)(or the yin in one's yang)

I personally look all around the casino, but my main concern is *"High Limits"*....High limit gaming is a different world for me because one light on the right machine can bring life- changing money to even a novice.! It's happened to me many times as I was playing a slot machine thinking thoughts and *Boom*; I got a light to go off and its 16k or 48k! To me that's life - changing money. I did not mention 75k or 63k. I was doing nothing more than playing a machine to the fullest! Those are real jackpots that I hit while gaming, using one of my methods that I'm writing about including Karma! Yes, I consider Karma as one of my greatest assets! As I approach any machine my mindset is on lights, but a lot of times you need credits first, so I slide in a 100 dollar bill on a ten dollar machine, that's ten credits. Playing Max bet, depending on the machine; in this case two credits is Max bet! keeping in mind, all it takes is one hit of max bet to get top dollar amount on any hit (check the machine you're playing to be sure you are aware of the cost for Max bet of that particular machine!).

Example
(These are situations that I have encountered a lot of times)

You hit for eight-hundred dollars, a lot of people take the money and run but not *TheSlotGuru*. Once I hit for three-hundred dollars or more on any given slot machine, I feel reassured that I have that money to play with *NOT* run with! (Unless that is what you are playing for, in that case great job!). With max credits bet, I have a couple different techniques. The first technique is, I hit Max bet when the reels stop. I hit it again quickly (fast play) repeat that three-five times, then if no light, I wait ten-fifteen seconds (slow play), then hit max bet again. Then every two-four seconds (quick ,but not supersonic fast play). To play or cash out depends on how many credits you have accumulated and how the machine has been paying out! Yes, there have been times when I had 2500 dollars worth of credits on the slot machine (with my style of gaming it happens a lot) and as I said before, it depends on how you are feeling on that given day. That's the gamble. But you have options. Option 1. Cash out and go get a light. Option 2. Play until you get to a certain amount, let's say 1800 dollars, and then cash out at

1500 dollars! (Because I never seem to leave on the mark that I set for myself) Option 3. I play all the way back down all the credits determined to get that light! To me it's almost like you're saying to the slot machine "I want more and I'm not going to settle for any thing less". So one of two things will happen at that point when you play all the way down from two- thousand five hundred - either you will hit a visible light (because two- thousand five hundred is a jackpot in accumulated credits but no lights come on because you did not get them on one spin ;you accumulated them ,therefore, you will not get taxed on that type of jackpot!) or you don't, and play all the credits back! I started with 100 dollars won up to two-thousand five hundred and playing for the light to come on I lose it all ., It has happened so many times to me….. I'm walking away scratching my scalp (because I have no hair) wondering what just happened ? Know when to stay or go! Trust me you will feel it! You must listen to your gut!

DO I OR DO I NOT USE MY PLAYERS' CARD?

Yes, yes, yes, I love my status of having the highest card level in the particular casino I'm playing . I think the slot machines sometimes give larger jackpots to high-level card holders (not proven - just my thoughts). Also most of the people I see that are regular big time winners use their cards, not to mention the food and rooms you get free for just using your card. And too many other things to list… massages, pool, recreation, gift shop, etc….did I say you earn points, that turn into cash ? So after you hit a jackpot while playing with your player's card, cash also goes on your player's card. Different casinos have different rules, so ask a casino employee to point you in the right direction, you'll be glad you did. Trust me!

WHAT'S ON MY MIND AS I'M PLAYING SLOTS?

Well to continue to be honest, all I'm thinking is lights… but I push that thought to the back of my mind as far back as I can push it! (Which isn't too far) and I try and think of all kinds of *positive* thoughts that keep me going through the night! And let me tell you about those lights, my friends, they come on when you least expect them to, most times! So I try to mentally not expect it all the time because it adds up to a lot of let downs and I don't like let downs but dealing with the casino full time has it's share. That's one of the main reasons I don't look at the screen because I don't like seeing two matching symbols and not three ahhhhhhhhhhhhhhhhhhhh! That feels like Mike Tyson just hit me in the stomach! But some how it all evens out because when I hit for 48k I felt great! Again, you have to be ready for the ups and downs, mentally tune out the *negative,* go with money you can afford to lose and have a great time *every time*! I also like to have mental dialog with people that are no longer in this world. Relatives, friends or close ones that have passed away, I find it to be very comforting, tranquilising and relaxing. And while I'm talking to my grandmother's spirit, a light comes on! It has happened too many times to count. I will not go off into extra- life experiences - that's another book! I will say the words I have with my relatives while I'm gaming are so nice and pleasant that it almost seems like they are right next to me. Then on comes a light! The words that are in this book can not be made up! I'm giving you my life experience inside the casino. Uncut and uncensored! You must read every word I write in this book to truly uncover my mindset as I'm in the casino, as I'm getting lights to go off, as I'm entertaining the other guests who wish it was them! Yes, this is my style of play. You can take away from or add to the styles you are reading to produce your own style of play, just keep absorbing the information I'm putting out and I'm sure your slot days are about to get a little nicer!

HOW I ACT AFTER A JACKPOT

There's nothing I hate more than a cocky winner! To me Karma is not on their side and I keep my distance. I have found out in my experiences at the casino that, even if a person make a light go off once or twice and they are not happy or if they don't tip or if they are just jerks in general, their night doesn't last too long. And sometime they even start talking to you, after they lose their bankroll or when they see *your* lights going off more often than theirs!

First, I thank whatever relatives' spirits I was talking to at the time, and then I smile through the whole process of getting paid. First, giving the slot attendants my license and social security card after that (some casinos take your license and social security card ,get the information they need ,then give your information back on the spot! reset the machine then have you do the spin off and you continue to play until you are paid [*Four Winds*]) or the walk to go get paid when they have your money ready. I must say it is a wonderful feeling as I'm escorted to the cashier's cage and my winnings are then counted out to me by the attendant at the counter. I'm smiling the entire way through even if its one-thousand two hundred dollars (Karma is something) then I tip depending on how long I had to wait to get paid. The longer the wait the lower the tip. Once I make it back to my machine, I then do my spin off, tip the slot attendant, and I'm right back at the slots. At that point you have the *option* of calling it a night. But not *TheSlotGuru*...

To me playing slots is a lot like life, you get out what you put in! Even me being a professional slot player, I still have to pay dues in the form of not hitting sometime! (At least that's what I call it!) and when that happens I get some food or relax at the hotel. Then either go home or get back in there! To me there's no two ways about it - either I'm in the casino to gamble or eat and sleep! I gamble first, then eat and sleep *maybe*!!!!!!!!!!!!!!

DIFFERENT MODES THAT THESLOTGURU PLAYS UNDER
(Playing styles and techniques I have learned over the years)

These are my definitions: I have never let this information out before now, so enjoy. You may have to re-read this book each time you're planning a trip to the casino. To your amazement, each time you read it, different parts of the book will get brighter to you. I promise.

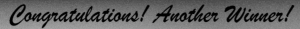

Congratulations! Another Winner!

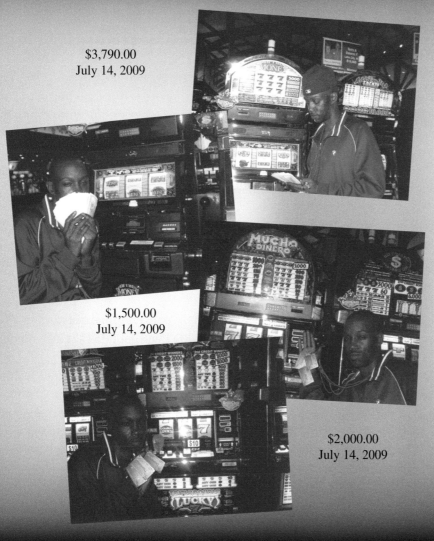

$3,790.00
July 14, 2009

$1,500.00
July 14, 2009

$2,000.00
July 14, 2009

Here are some playing techniques I use and have observed over the years.

1. Fast play mode- fast play on one slot is hitting the button in two-four sec intervals (I told you this earlier, remember). And that's when I'm playing one machine!

2. Slow play mode- hitting the button in ten sec intervals all the time. No changing up - just straight play at ten sec intervals or more per hit of the button. (This one is too slow for me but I have seen people play this technique with some success) Also it's good to use this with fast or moderate play. Say if you're on fast play mode and you hit the max bet button four times on the fifth time I pause, *Slow Play* one hit of the max credit button then go back to fast play mode. That's just one way of putting together different styles, my friends.

3. Moderate play mode-hitting the button between five and ten sec intervals. This is a vital part of my personal formula as well as fast play! Because I have thoughts going on in my mind as I play, I'm not hitting the button as quick and I slip into moderate time frame.

    I combine fast-play with moderate-play, when I'm playing one slot machine. (This is rare! Because I hardly ever play only one slot, I will get into that in a moment!)

4. Going with your gut mode- yes I said it, one of my most successful techniques ever! Once I come into the casino, I have an instant head rush, my heart starts pounding. It's a feeling that I love to feel, that's when I get first get there, but once I start gaming after no lights for a period of time (normally around ten minutes) that feeling quickly leaves, my friends, but on the other hand, to combine that feeling with a light going off on the first game you play is unbelievable! (This has happened numerous times to TheSlotGuru to say the least! Not bragging just letting you know, it can happen to you also, my friends). Trust me!

**THESE ARE SOME OF THE DIFFERENT TYPES OF PLAYERS
THAT THESLOTGURU HAS NOTICED AT THE CASINOS.**

1. Penny-pinch-playing - this style, I personally think is the worst of all for *ME*. These are the casino patrons that come in the casino and just play one credit on one line at the slots and really be expecting to win something... I smile, speak if we make eye contact and observe the machine they are on and if I'm around after they leave, I go right behind them and set a light off. (True story)

2. The cautious player - they watch you from far and wait until you get off, they observe exactly how much cash you are putting in the machine, how long you've played it and soon as you leave, here they come. It's best not to look back. And reverse the table if you can...play some machines they were on if you ever see them play.

3. Ghost players- these are the players that always seem to be there to congratulate you when you hit a light, but again no one never actually see them playing. Strange people!

4. The card/slot player- they play the tables full-time but do a little moon lighting on the slots...any winnings they get on slots they put back at the table....all you have to do is observe them, sometime they are looking at a slot machine and trying to get to it but can't leave the card table... use your sense to observe what game they want to play and go to that slot and play it a few rounds... you may be very pleasantly surprised! Trust me!

5. The always hitters- the people that always seem to hit. Good idea to observe them as you're gaming if they are in your area. Watch the games they play , take mental notes and play them at your leisure if you feel like it...you will soon be one of them, the always- hitters! Trust me...

WHICH BILLS DO I THINK ARE BEST TO USE?

I personally have played with all bills… 10s seem to make me tired because I'm constantly feeding the machine and that gets a little tiring… 50s ,people say are bad luck and they may be right because I have rarely hit a jackpot with 50s !!!!!!!!I think that playing with twenty dollar bills are good, but I have to put five in at a time to equal 100 dollars. That's not too bad, but still kind of ho hum! (Boring to me) I mainly play with 100 dollar bills and always have some 20s on hand to play with as well…every one's bankroll is different, but I favor the 100 dollar bills and that's what I play with mostly.

HOW I GET ANNOYING PEOPLE AWAY FROM ME,
WITHOUT GETTING THE CASINO INVOLVED

First off, let me say that everyone that talks to you are not annoying. Only the ones that are bothersome to you…these are the ones that want to just sit there and talk about nothing while looking over your shoulder hoping you lose…. You can take two simple routes to get rid of these pests that seem to bring bad luck, first, if you have a cell phone and the person is still there just whip out your cell phone and act like you answered it, look directly at the person that's being an annoyance and simply say "good luck I got to take this call"; at that point, stop play and walk a few feet away, your money in the machine is okay, the casinos have more cameras than you can shake a stick at. So they know that's your machine. Ninety- nine percent of the time they will leave! If they don't , then you simply look at them and let them know you do like being watched while you're gaming… that's that they're gone…(most of the time if it gets this far, the slot attendants that you tipped will see what's going on with out you saying a word and will shoo them away! They take care of you; you just make sure you take care of them once you get a light on!

Congratulations! Another Winner!

$2,840.00
July 14, 2009

$5,100.00
July 14, 2009

$2,500.00
July 14, 2009

$1,600.00
July 14, 2009

HOW I CHOOSE WHICH MACHINE TO PLAY...

As I'm walking around in high stakes, I'm also looking at the payout of the machine and normally I float in the direction of the highest paying slot machines, but with Karma and observing, I relax my mind and walk up to any game that interests me and some games that don't interest me and I start gaming... no clues to look for, no magic tricks! I'm not telling you, I look at a screen and by the combination on the screen that's what determines if I play that machine or not! No way, shape or form do I go by that nonsense. I have never walked up and won money because of a combination that's on the screen. (I have however played a machine that had two sevens showing out of three but I didn't get a light! But that doesn't mean if you do play a machine with the symbols showing you will not get a light. (I'm telling you my story) Most of the time, I'm not looking at the screen so, I couldn't tell you what's on the screen! Regardless of what the screen shows, if you want to play that particular game, then go ahead and play it, Max bet it! You will also run into people within the casino that think they know everything about every jackpot that's been hit for the past years on every machine in the casino!!!! I do in fact listen to their information, but it really holds *no* water whatsoever on my gaming! Sometimes when they tell me a person put fifteen grand in a machine and got nothing out, that's worth a try if I feel like it; but it's times when I'm playing a machine and a person walks up and tells me, someone hit on the machine I had been playing on earlier, I look them in their eyes and say thank you for the information! To me that is negative and it holds *no* weight with me....in most cases I get a light on that very machine! (Once you get in good with Karma your entire casino experiences will change)!

ADVANCE PLAY
(one of my specialties)

To me advance play is when you play multiple machines at one time, my friends. THIS is what I do, again without a nice bank roll you can not use this technique. But that's no problem, your bank roll will be larger if you just comprehend my information that I'm putting in this book. You will be just fine again, with some moving around….playing two or three machines at once is a delight for me because I don't like watching the screen anyway and unless you're playing two machines that are side by side or that particular playing mode you are playing in, for example,; if you are playing two - end machines right across from each other and you play slow mode, which then you will have time to watch the screen and see the outcome on both games you are playing! Even if you play three games at once in slow mode, you will have time to watch your outcome of all games! Example two, however, is a little more constant movement -involved! This is my mode and this is my gaming most of the time. So you can see why I quit my job because I was tired night in night out with this type of play………………on most nights, I may start off with two machines; I usually never play one unless my money is getting low…and once I get a light to come on, then I'm off and going in a fast mode- constant meaning….while I'm waiting for the slot attendant to bring me back a 15000 jackpot on one machine, I hit another for fourteen-thousand before they paid me for the first one…yes this happened to me quit often that's why I love what I call 'constant play meaning I'm playing while I'm waiting to get paid . I'm still hitting Max bet on a machine that is next to the machine that I hit the jackpot on, so while they are counting my money to me at the machine, I sometime still hit Max bet on the machine next to it, if I can reach it(some casinos pay you at the machine if your jackpot is five-thousand or less, depending on the casino!) I play other machines when I'm waiting to get paid, so when they come back I have another light off or two or three lights going off at one time! That's my fast mode; these same lights will go off in slow or moderate mode as well! On good nights I play seven (7) to ten (10) slots at the same time. My play mode is fast which means that it's not stopping for me until my body gets tired! I have played rows at a time or two rows at a time or I have played sections at a time. I'm getting older but in my hey day, I used to tell people I was at the gym because I was constantly on my feet and yes my feet get tired after eight or nine hours or more of constant play. It has been times when I was on fast mode for about thirteen hours the lights were going off like crazy. My arm was so tired from me raising it up all night just to get paid….I think I raised my arms over fifty times that night. My whole body gets tired, that's why it's good to choose a casino with great hotels, rest up and you will feel like a new person when you get up….

WINNING PERCENTAGE OF A MACHINE

A thing like a winning percentage of a machine to me just doesn't matter much because even the machine with a low percentage still hits sometime. Who knows when that last time was? I say that to say do your gaming, I in particular enjoy playing hard to hit slots or should I say the slots that guests deem to be hard to hit... more of a challenge for TheSlotGuru and when those so- called hard hitting machines hit the payout life could be changing ,my friends, you never know unless you play it!!!!!

WHAT IS GOING ON INSIDE THE SLOT MACHINE? WHAT MAKES IT TICK?
HOW CAN YOU GET AN EDGE ON SLOTS? (here is the way I see it)

Let me say this loud and clear...I do not go inside a casino thinking of nothing more than a light... that light can be 1200 dollars or a million dollars, all I ask my farther for is lights... to know how a machine or when a machine will hit. I personally think it can not be done and if it could be done it's wrong and with wrongness comes bad Karma and with that comes a rough life, my friends...playing by the rules make gambling worth while for a guy like myself. The thing is this, the machines are going to hit, I don't know when or where, but I can say I will play my best when I'm there and I want you to do the same. And if anyone says they know how to beat the casino you say 'Show ME'! They will talk a good game, but when it comes down to it ,don't waste your time or energy…..money will be given to you as you will be successful playing the slots like a pro…

WHAT TIME OF DAY DO I GO TO THE CASINO MOST OFTEN?

I used to think going at certain times of the day and certain days of the week would influence the machine to hit. For example: I used to think that the machine only hit on weekends or the machine only hit in the daytime or I thought the machines only hit right after they were changed or before it was time to get changed. Yes, my mind clicks more than a stop watch! Until over years of gaming and observing and winning and more observing until I can honestly say to you my friends that anytime is a good time to hit a jackpot! Sometime I go on Mondays or Tuesdays or Wednesdays or Thursdays or Fridays or Saturday or Sunday (you see where I'm going with this don't you?)(Anytime is a good time)! Most of the time, I go between 10p.m. and 5a.m., but that's really not saying much. I stay ten or thirty -six hours sometime, really, starting off with a bankroll of three-thousand to four-thousand dollars (remember we are talking about *Me*, if you want to go with a smaller bankroll that's fine because remember, all it takes is one good light and any light is a good light, my friends!) ....

I'M NOT GOING TO TELL YOU, THAT YOU WILL HIT A JACKPOT ON EVERY TRIP!
(I ALSO WILL NOT TELL YOU THAT YOU WON'T!)

There is absolutely no way I can tell you or guarantee that you will hit a light every time you step into the casino; that would make me a liar! What I will say and stand behind is this book and my style and techniques that I am explaining. If you read and more importantly really comprehend what you are reading in this book, then your mindset will change and yes, your luck will also change!

ONE THING THAT GOES THRU' MY MIND AS I LOSE AND LOSE BAD.

To continue to be as real as I possibly can, as I'm having a bad night at the slots, for me bad only comes in one of three ways! 1) I get a few lights as soon as I get there, playing moderate mode and lose it all back before I get to high limits! (A bad start) Yes, I play certain high paying penny, nickels, dimes and quarter machines. (On a Max bet, it may be fifteen bucks on a penny, if I change the denomination to five cent on the same machine it is a seventy-five bucks Max bet) (These games are on the floor before you even reach high stakes and if you're not careful, these will prevent you making it to high stakes. Be careful, my friends but they do pay out! Real nice! Remember to observe). When I first get to the casino as I'm making my way to high limits and I get a few lights to come on before I make my way to high limits is a great start! 2) To make it to high limits with the same size bank roll or better than when I entered the casino, instantly get some lights to come on in high stakes!!! So far so good, right? Right? 3) The bad part is I don't leave when I'm ahead! (And still don't) and when I do leave, some twenty-four hours later, sometimes it's not good, my friends... these are the facts. This is when you make your own choice, my friends...remember to go to the casino with what you can afford to lose! If you go there with that mindset, your trip will be more enjoyable! If this scenario ever happens to you, you are now prepared! (Remember in the beginning of the book, I said leave when you're ahead, and that's what is on my mind as I'm getting my rear end handed to me on a platter!)

HOW I ACT AND WHAT I DO, AFTER I LOSE AT THE CASINO?

As my last few credits that I'm playing with for that trip wind down and I know it's pretty much a done deal for this trip! It's very important for me to smile (as much as I can) and speak on my way out, as I do when I get there! If I'm hungry I go and eat free because I used my player's card as I was playing. Most of the time I do go and eat, relax and wind down. I do not stand around digging in my nose or looking at other people play or telling every person that's playing a machine I hit on that "I hit on that machine"....no no no! To be a true gamer you have to accept losing just like winning! Karma is such a beautiful thing and there is a blessing in everything in life, my friends (that's just how I feel) you just have to stay thinking positive, it has not failed me yet! If you master the art of leaving once your ahead, you will be fine...that's a tough art to master... But not impossible!

HOW DO I FEEL AFTER A BAD LOSS ON MY WAY HOME?
(IF I DRIVE HOME)

To me a *Bad* loss is when I should have left but didn't.. I would be ahead by 10k or 30k and don't leave. When it's all said and done I lose and go home saying I should have left when I was ahead. Ninety-five percent of the time I'm ahead. I love driving and being on the road, on the way home is very tranquil, playing nice soft music and relaxing. Of course, I'm tired from gaming. No matter how long I'm there. It's always a work out! If I get too tired on my way home, I pull over in a public area and take a nap, wake up and take my badly bruised bottom home! Once I make it home, I get around family, and look at reality and smile and laugh with loved ones. I try to look out for everyone, so when something happens to *TheSlotGuru*, I get comfort in helping others and they have no idea that they (my family and friends ,guys at the barber shop) are helping me to feel better! (Karma is more than a game to me, my friends ,it's my life! Don't only treat people nice when you win, treat them nice when you lose as well. That's my story and I'm sticking to it!

JUST TO LET YOU KNOW HOW UNPREDICTABLE THE CASINOS ARE.....

True story: as I was exiting a casino, I always play all the cash I have with me, so on my last two-hundred dollars I observed a one-dollar machine, but the Max bet was forty-five dollars. I hit for ten grand! that's right, then I left the machine and came back after about fifteen minutes, put a hundred dollar bill and won sixty-eight thousand dollars....I went from two-hundred dollars to seventy-eight thousand in less than thirty minutes !!!!! I still get a rush when I think about it! That's why I don't give up!

HOW DO I HONESTLY FEEL ABOUT MY JOB AS A PROFESSIONAL GAMBLER?

I love it, it's exhilarating for me. Yes, I have bad days but the good ones far out weigh the bad ones… it's all about my mindset and how I am in my world, life is not just the casino!!!!!!! I don't go every night… when the time is right, I'm off to work!! I love being a gamer! As I walk in I never know how the night will end. I never know how much I may win. The thrill of the unknown is awesome, You have to love it or hate it? And if you want good Karma, you do not hate anything, right?

HOW DO I FEEL ABOUT THE CASINOS

I personally think that the casinos are a business to make money…I also know they give out winnings as well (millions per month, I don't know the exact amount but it's a lot), my job is to get my share from any casino I want. If I make 100 trips to the casino, I get ahead (ahead meaning more cash than I came with) ninety-five times out of 100. (Leaving can be hard because of the fun and the rush from those lights!) I have never had a problem at the casino with getting paid any of my jackpots I have hit…they never made me wait too long after a big hit…forty-thousand…fifty-thousand…those types of big hits, my friends. And remember you're on camera from the time you're in the parking lot until you step in and beyond. I love the fact that I don't have to look over my shoulders. The casinos give me that comfort when I'm there. So to me, the casino is one of the safest places to be! When you are dealing with millions of dollars a day, as many casinos do, I go in and don't want to cause any problems…. I'm there to win and enjoy the entertainment and use my card because sometime I think the casinos let their cardholders win more. That's my take(haven't been proven- that's just what I think sometimes), if you think about it- that's how the casinos know when their friend is playing and they track your style of play, bets and the lights worth the big bucks come to the card holder a lot in my experiences at the slots …..Trust me! (Observe)

Congratulations! Another Winner!

$2,400.00 &
$1,500.00
July 14, 2009

$4,800.00
July 14, 2009

$2,040.00
July 14, 2009

$2,390.00
July 14, 2009

Congratulations! Another Winner!

$1,320.00
July 14, 2009

$18,000.00
July 14, 2009

$1,250.00
July 14, 2009

$1,640.00
July 14, 2009

MY GUIDE TO YOU LEARNING FROM MY UPS AND DOWNS..........

ONE OF THE MANY REASONS I WANTED TO PUT MY 19 YEARS OF EXPERIENCE IN THE CASINO IN THIS BOOK IS TO SEE IF I CAN SHOW PEOPLE EXACTLY WHAT I DO, EXACTLY HOW I THINK, HOW I MOVE! YOU MUST READ EVERY LINE, GO TO THE CASINO COME BACK TIP ME. READ IT AGAIN! AND YOU SHOULD BE LAUGHING PRETTY HARD, BECAUSE YOU NOW REALIZE, I HIT SO MANY NAILS ON THE HEAD! IT TOOK ME 19YEARS TO PUT THIS COLLABORATION TOGETHER. AND THE BOOK ISN'T THICK FOR A REASON MY FRIENDS....IN THIS BOOK I DIDN'T WANT WASTED WORDS TO PUT YOU TO SLEEP WHILE YOU READ MY MANUAL, I'M NOT TALKING ABOUT WHAT I DON'T KNOW, I'M TALKING ABOUT WHAT I DO KNOW AND THAT'S SLOTS, I WILL ONLY HOPE AND PRAY THAT YOU YOURSELF GET LIGHTS TO GO OFF AND IF YOU FOLLOW MY LEAD YOU WILL BE FINE! IF YOU GET ONE LIGHT IT PAID FOR THIS BOOK AND THE PRICELESS INFORMATION THAT'S IN IT! (UNLESS THEY CHARGED YOU 1200 DOLLARS FOR THE BOOK). AS I TOLD YOU HOW I ACT WHEN I'M UP AND DOWN LEARN FROM IT! EMBRACE IT! BECAUSE YOU WILL HIT MY FRIEND! TRUST ME!!!!!!

PUT TOGETHER YOUR OWN STYLES
FROM MY OWN TECHNIQUES AND STRATEGIES ...

I would like for you to experiment with your own time formula and different modes of play... no two styles are the same, my friends, as long as you are aware of that and everything else that I covered in this book, then you have my mindset going into the casino.....the book is small enough to read five times over! I'm a firm believer in having a great casino experience even if I lose on that trip...

YOU CAN USE MY STYLE AND METHODS ON ANY MACHINE FROM THE PENNY MACHINES UPTO BUT NOT LIMITED TO THE HUNDRED DOLLAR MACHINES AND BEYOND...

That's right any machine in the casino, you can use my styles and methods on because that's what I do. I favor the "high limits" but as I said before, I play one cent and five cent and twenty-five cent machines as I'm making my way to high limits! Remember what you read in this book, my friends… it may cost you a jackpot if you don't!

THE REMAINING PAGES IS A SMALL PORTFOLIO OF SOME OF MY WORK/WINNINGS AT THE CASINOS. I HAVE REPEATED THINGS IN THIS BOOK ON PURPOSE… IT'S CALLED REPETITION AND IT'S AN EFFECTIVE TOOL TO LEARN WITH…AS WILL SEE… I DON'T KNOW YOU AND YOU DON'T KNOW ME BUT SOMEHOW I FEEL CONNECTED TO THE PEOPLE THAT ARE READING MY BOOK AND FOLLOWING SOME OF MY SIMPLE BUT EFFECTIVE STRATEGIES. I TAKE NOTHING FOR GRANTED, MY FRIENDS…WHEN I GO GO THE CASINO IT'S A JOB FOR ME, I HAVE TO WIN TO SURVIVE AND TO ME THERE IS NO ROOM FOR SECOND PLACE! IN THIS CASE SECOND PLACE IS BETTING ANYTHING LESS THAN 'MAX BET' ON ANY MACHINE THAT I PLAY ON, NO EXCEPTIONS…I ENJOY TREATING PEOPLE WELL EVEN IF I DON'T LEAVE THE CASINO WITH ANY MONEY THAT DAY! THAT'S WHY IT'S VERY IMPORTANT TO PLAY WITH YOUR PLAYERS' CARD, SO IF YOU DO GET BROKE OR REACH YOUR MAX FOR THE DAY THAT'S OKAY…YOUR CARD WILL FEED YOU AND GIVE YOU HOTEL ACCOMMODATIONS! AND DID I SAY FOOD??????????????I CHOOSE YOUR CASINOS CAREFULLY MY, FRIENDS…TO BE FRANK IF I LOSE ON THREE STRAIGHT TRIPS, THEN I TAKE A HIATUS FROM THAT PARTICULAR CASINO… UNLESS YOU USE THE CASINOS AS YOUR MAIN SOURCE OF INCOME LIKE I DO, THEN YOU SHOULD NOT ENCOUNTER SUCH DROUGHTS AS I HAVE. BUT DON'T HOLD ME TO THAT, MY FRIENDS, THAT'S JUST MY MINDSET. YOU MUST REMEMBER IT'S STILL A GAMBLE ,MY FRIENDS…DON'T YOU LOVE IT? NO, WELL YOU WILL, ONCE YOU GET A LIGHT TO COME ON, ON A CONSISTENT BASIS… DON'T BE GREEDY.ONCE THE LIGHT OR LIGHTS COME ON TAKE YOUR WINNINGS,ENJOY YOURSELF GIVE SOME AWAY… I ALWAYS FIND IT GREAT TO DO SOMETHING OR GIVE PEOPLE MONEY THAT'S NOT EXPECTING IT…LIKE THE LADY IN FRONT OF ME AT THE GAS STATION; SHE HAD A FIVE

OR TEN DOLLAR BILL AND I JUST PAID IT FOR HER AND TOLD HER TO HAVE A BLESSED DAY AND SHE WAS VERY THANKFUL AND THAT MADE IT ALL WORTH WHILE.... THE LOOK ON THEIR FACES ARE OVERWHELMING. THE POWER OF GIVING IS ONE OF THOSE THINGS WHERE YOU HAVE TO DO IT, TO TRULY APPRECIATE IT!

AND IF YOU GIVE ENOUGH, EXPECTING NOTHING IN RETURN FROM THE PEOPLE THAT YOU MAY HELP, MY FRIEND, WILL PAY YOU A VISIT PERSONALLY!!! THAT I PROMISE...HER NAME IS "KARMA" AND SHE IS AS NICE AS SHE COMES. SHE DOESN'T TALK MUCH, BUT THE THINGS SHE DOES SPEAKS VOLUMES, MY FRIEND...AND IF YOU ARE DOING GOOD THINGS, THEN YOU MAY HAVE MET KARMA ALREADY. SHE IS A REAL FRIEND AND SHE IS ALWAYS AROUND WHEN YOU NEED HER. AND WHEN SHE TAKES CARE OF YOU BY ALLOWING YOU TO HIT SOME LIGHTS, MAKE SURE YOU DO SOMETHING FOR SOMEONE ELSE.....

I REMEMBER ONE DAY I WAS AT THE CASINO AND IT WAS A GREAT DAY FOR ME. LIGHTS WERE GOING OFF ALL OVER THE PLACE! I WON WELL OVER 100 THOUSAND DOLLARS THAT TRIP (WHICH IS AN EXTREMELY RARE EVENT) WHICH LASTED FOR ONE DAY! A BUNCH OF HITS... FIVE-THOUSAND, SEVEN-THOUSAND, EIGHTEEN-THOUSAND... AS I WOULD HIT I WOULD GIVE SOMEONE SOME MONEY, YES TOTAL STRANGERS MOSTLY, IF NOT ALL. PEOPLE WAS HAVING A BAD DAY WE ALL KNOW ABOUT THOSE BAD DAYS! BUT WE ALL DON'T KNOW ABOUT A STRANGER THAT JUST HAD FORTUNE IMPACT HIS OR HER LIFE. AND THEY JUST GIVE SOME OF IT TO WHO THEY WANT WITH NO EXPLANATION, IS A GREAT FEELING, ALMOST AS GOOD AS THE JACKPOT ITSELF!(I SAID ALMOST!) THROUGH OUT THAT ONE-DAY EVENT, I MUST HAVE GIVEN AWAY ONE OR TWO THOUSAND. ALL THAT KIND OF DREW PEOPLE TO HIGH LIMITS AND PEOPLE COME WHERE THE LIGHTS ARE! I ASSISTED PEOPLE THAT DAY WITH MAX BETTING ADVICE AND KARMA

ADVICE; THE ONES THAT LISTENED WERE GETTING LIGHTS AND THE ONES THAT DIDN'T WERE WATCHING THEM GET LIGHTS.(TRUE STORY)THE DAY ENDED FOR ME BY HITTING A JACKPOT FOR FORTY-FIVE THOUSAND DOLLARS. I WALK UP TO A FAMILY OF EIGHT OR NINE AND GAVE THEM ALL 100 BUCKS EACH. (WHAT A FEELING THAT WAS!). THEY ASKED WHY AND I SIMPLY SAID THAT I JUST HIT AND I HAVE TO DO SOMETHING GOOD. THE GRANDMOTHER STARTED TO CRY AS DID I. IT IS A GREAT FEELING, I CANT STRESS THAT ENOUGH. NO LONG EXTENDED DISCUSSION IS NEEDED! THAT'S THE WHOLE THING .YOU DO IT FROM YOUR HEART AND YOUR CASINO TRIPS WILL CHANGE FOR THE BETTER! IF YOU THINK HOW YOU LIVE YOUR LIFE AND HOW YOU TREAT OTHERS DON'T HAVE ANY INFLUENCE ON YOUR LUCK AT THE CASINO, THINK AGAIN ,MY FRIENDS...TRUST ME. (AGAIN! THIS WAS A RARE OCCURRENCE, YES IT HAS HAPPENED TO ME BEFORE, BUT IT'S JUST NOT AN EVERYDAY EVENT TO WIN THAT TYPE OF CASH. YOU MUST BE REALISTIC! BUT IT HAS HAPPENED TO ME AND CAN HAPPEN TO YOU, MY FRIENDS)! ON THAT PARTICULAR DAY, I WAS PLAYING FAST MODE ON MULTIPLE MACHINES, ALL DAY LONG. I KEPT THE ATTENDANTS BUSY AND THEY WERE SERVING ME EXPEDITIOUSLY! YES, MY TIPS WERE HELPING THAT TRIP!

MY LOCAL CASINOS MADE ME RICH....

YES, THIS IS TRUE MY FRIENDS; I HAVE YET TO GO TO VEGAS OR ATL CITY. IF MY STYLES AND METHODS ARE GOOD IN MICHIGAN, I WONDER HOW GREAT THEY WILL WORK IN THOSE PLACES WHERE I HEAR THEY HAVE ONE -THOUSAND DOLLAR SLOTS...WOW! I'M SURE KARMA WILL BE WITH ME...SHE ALWAYS IS...AND SHE WILL ALWAYS BE WITH YOU AS LONG AS YOU LIVE THE RIGHT WAY, MY FRIENDS...NONE OF US IS PERFECT BUT IT IS UP TO YOU TO MAKE YOURSELF A GREAT PERSON AND THAT WILL TRANSPIRE INTO THE GAMING AREA! I WISH I COULD SEE THE LOOK ON SOME OF YOUR FACES WHEN THOSE LIGHTS START GOING OFF

ON A MORE CONSTANT BASIS. I'M PROUD OF YOU ALREADY! CONGRATULATIONS! IF YOU CAN VISUALISE IT, YOU CAN DO IT….TRUST ME!

AT THIS TIME I WOULD LIKE TO THANK THE CASINOS THAT GAVE ME MY GREATEST GAMING EXPERIENCE, THE CASINOS THAT I'M ABOUT TO NAME HAVE NOT PAID ME TO MENTION THEM IN THIS BOOK, NOR DO I WORK FOR ANY OF THESE CASINOS. I'M NOTHING MORE THAN ONE PERSON OUT OF MANY WHO HAS WON MILLIONS AT THE CASINO. THE DIFFERENCE WITH ME IS, I HAVE TAKEN YOU INSIDE MY MIND AND TOLD YOU WHAT'S ON MY MIND AT DIFFERENT MOMENTS. THANK YOU, MOTOR CITY CASINO IN DETROIT, MI., GREEKTOWN CASINO IN DETROIT, MI., MGM CASINO IN DOWNTOWN DETROIT, MI., CEASERS OF WINDSOR,CANADA, SOARING EAGLE CASINO AND RESORT IN MOUNT PLEASANT, MICHIGAN AND FOUR WINDS CASINO RESORT IN NEW BUFFALO,MICHIGAN. THANK YOU ALL FOR THE EXPERIENCES A PERSON CAN DREAM OF. I'M GOING ON A TOUR OF VEGAS AND ATL CITY AND OTHERS TO SEE THE DIFFERENT EXPERIENCES. THANK YOU ALL FOR BEING TOP NOTCH ESTABLISHMENTS! THANK YOU AGAIN…AND DID I SAY ALL OF YOUR FOOD IS DELICIOUS? IT'S DELICIOUS! NOTHING IS BETTER THAN GAMING ALL NIGHT, ON YOUR FEET ALL NIGHT AND HAVE A WONDERFUL TIME SLEEPING IN A CLEAN ROOM AND THE SPA SERVICE FOR THE ONES THAT HAVE IT, IT IS A GREAT TENSION DIMINISH-ER! THANKS FOR PAYING ME THE CASH JACKPOTS WITH SMILES ON YOUR FACES. (FOR ALL THAT APPLY)….THANKS!

AND LASTLY, I WOULD LIKE TO LEAVE YOU WITH A FEW WORDS OF WISDOM FROM MY LIFE/ CASINO EXPERIENCES.YOU HAVE TO PUT OUT POSITIVE ENERGY TO ACQUIRE POSITIVE RESULTS! READ THIS BOOK ENOUGH YOU WILL SEE AND UNCOVER CERTAIN THINGS THAT ARE NOT VISIBLE TO THE NAKED EYE. THE ONE THAT CAN READ AND UNDERSTAND EVERYTHING

I'M SAYING. THEN YOU WILL LEARN OUR PERSONAL SUCCESS IN LIFE DEPENDS ON HOW WE TREAT OTHERS, IN OUR LIFE, FAMILY AND STRANGERS. YOU ARE YOUR OWN JUDGE ON WHAT YOU DEEM TO BE RIGHT. YOU ARE IN CONTROL OF YOUR LIFE AND TIME WILL COME FOR YOU TO HELP OUT OR DO NICE THINGS FOR PEOPLE. THANK YOU FOR PURCHASING MY BOOK, I WISH YOU GUYS THE BEST OF LUCK ON YOUR GAMING EXPERIENCE! PLEASE RE- READ THIS BOOK AND MAKE SURE YOU GET IT AND ONCE YOU DO GET IT YOU MAY EXPERIENCE SOME FORM OF A REVELATION, DON'T BE ALARMED IT'S JUST OUR GOOD FRIEND "KARMA" WORKING YOU OVER IN A POSITIVE WAY AND PLEASE NO MATTER WHAT YOU DO, NEVER, EVER "GO LOOKING FOR YOUR BLESSINGS" OR SEARCHING FOR KARMA! MEANING, DON'T DO SOMETHING FOR SOMEONE JUST TO HAVE SOMETHING GOOD HAPPEN TO YOU! IT MUST BE DONE FROM YOUR HEART, NO MATTER HOW SMALL OR BIG, MY FRIENDS. IN MY PURSUIT OF SLOT RICHES, I TRY AND BE AS HUMBLE AS POSSIBLE, IT GOES A VERY LONG WAY. TRUST ME! JULY 30, 2009

NEWS FLASH!!!!!!!!!! *I JUST RETURNED HOME FROM A WONDERFUL TIME AT THE SOARING EAGLE CASINO AND RESORT IN MOUNT PLEASANT MI... I AM A DIAMOND CARD HOLDER! IT TAKES 400,000 POINTS TO MAKE DIAMOND. I TOLD YOU THAT, SO YOU CAN UNDERSTAND THE NEXT THING I'M ABOUT TO SAY. I PICKED UP MY NEW DIAMOND CARD ON SATURDAY JULY 11, 2009. ONCE IT WAS OVER AND DONE WITH (MY TRIP) WHICH ENDED ON JULY 13,2009, TWO DAYS LATER, I ACCUMULATED OVER 500,000 POINTS TO CONTINUE MY DIAMOND STATUS FOR ANOTHER SIX MONTHS. YES,YOU READ IT CORRECTLY MY FRIENDS. I DID OVER 200,000 DOLLARS IN WINNINGS IN TWO DAYS ON A WIDE VARIETY OF SLOTS RANGING FROM THE PENNY MACHINES TO THE TWENTY-FIVE-DOLLAR SLOTS. I HAD A BLAST BY DOING EXACTLY WHAT I WROTE IN THIS BOOK.WOW! WHAT A WONDERFUL RIDE THAT WAS.*

Congratulations! Another Winner!

$2,000.00
July 14, 2009

$1,200.00
July 14, 2009

$1,500.00
July 14, 2009

$5,000.00
July 14, 2009

AND LASTLY, I HAVE HEARD THINGS ON THE CASINO FLOOR ABOUT THE CASINOS, SUCH AS "THEY (THE CASINO) NEVER LET ANYONE BLACK HIT" WELL, YET ANOTHER MYTH! THE SLOT MACHINES HAVE NO EYEBALLS SO THEREFORE CAN NOT DETERMINE WHAT COLOUR OR GENDER YOU ARE. AND FOR THE PEOPLE OUT THERE THAT THINK THE CASINOS ARE RACIST ,YOU NEED TO LOSE THAT BAD KARMA AND CHANGE YOUR WAY OF THINKING AND I GUARANTEE YOU, YOUR CASINO EXPERIENCE WILL CHANGE...IN CLOSING I WOULD LIKE TO ADD...WE HAVE A BLACK PRESIDENT AND THERE IS NO WAY POSSIBLE HE COULD HAVE BEEN ELECTED WITHOUT WHITE VOTES! THAT BEING SAID FOR THE GAMERS THAT NEVER HIT AT THE SLOTS AND BLAME THE CASINOS FOR THEIR LOSS BECAUSE OF COLOUR, GET REAL, BECAUSE IF YOU DON'T, LIFE WILL PASS YOU BY AND SO WILL I. IF YOU GO IN THERE WITH THE RIGHT MINDSET AS I STATED YOU WILL BE A WINNER JUST LIKE ME... TRUST ME.... HERE IS MY WEBSITE FOR THE GAMERS THAT WANT TO GIVE THESLOTGURU A TIP AFTER THE JACKPOTS ROLL IN. (www.theslotguru.com) REMEMBER KARMA! YES, FOR EVERYONE THAT IS READING MY BOOK, WE ARE CONNECTED BY SPIRITS. AND YOU WILL BE A MIRROR IMAGE OF ME GOING INTO ALL TYPES OF CASINOS ALL OVER THE WORLD.

I WILL NOT KNOW WHEN YOU HIT BUT IF YOU DON'T INCORPORATE THESLOTGURU IN YOUR GAMING LIFE, THEN YOUR KARMA SHALL CHANGE AS YOU WILL SEE. WE ARE GAMBLERS AND WE PLEDGE THAT WE WILL TAKE CARE OF THE PERSON THAT HELPS TAKE YOUR GAMING TO THE HIGHEST LEVEL. THAT'S ME, THESLOTGURU I HAVE JUST PUT OUT INFORMATION THAT'S GOING TO CHANGE THOUSANDS IF NOT MILLIONS OF LIVES. THIS BOOK IS ONLY FOR THE SERIOUS GAMERS. TAKE CARE OF THE PERSON THAT BROUGHT YOU THE INFORMATION. BECAUSE I'M SURE YOU WILL DO WELL SO I EXPECT MY CUT. THAT'S KARMA AND YOU ARE OBLIGATED TO LOOK OUT FOR THE ONE THAT LOOKS OUT FOR YOU. IF NOT' YOUR KARMA WILL CHANGE. TRUST ME...

ONCE AGAIN THANK YOU FOR THE PURCHASE OF MY BOOK AND ACCEPT YOUR WINNINGS THAT'S COMING YOUR WAY. CONTACT MY WEB SITE FOR ORDERING INFORMATION...I WILL BE SETTING UP A SITE FOR THOSE THAT WANT IMMEDIATE QUESTIONS ANSWERED! THIS IS A NEW GENERATION OF GAMING. YOU'RE LOOKING AT MY STATISTICS, NOW I ASK YOU, DO YOU WANT TO BE ON MY TEAM???? WELCOME TO MY WORLD OF GAMING!!! BOTTOM LINE: GET READY TO GET PAID! TRUST ME.

I hope to say one more thing, I want to be rich so that I can be able to give away all my money to help people because you can't die with it, my friend.

Congratulations! Another Winner!

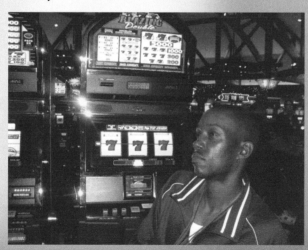

$3,000.00
July 14, 2009

Congratulations! Another Winner!

$1,250.00
July 14, 2009

$3,200.00
July 14, 2009

$5,500.00
July 14, 2009

$1,600.00
July 14, 2009

Congratulations! Another Winner!

$5,000.00
July 14, 2009

$1,500.00
July 14, 2009

$3,000.00
July 14, 2009

$1,250.00
July 14, 2009

Congratulations! Another Winner!

$1,200.00
July 14, 2009

$2,400.00 &
1,500.00
July 14, 2009

Congratulations! Another Winner!

$2,390.00
July 14, 2009

$1,56.00
July 14, 2009

Congratulations! Another Winner!

$2,920.00
July 14, 2009

$1,720.00
July 14, 2009

Congratulations! Another Winner!

$1,300.00
July 14, 2009

$3,790.00
July 14, 2009

Printed in the United States
By Bookmasters